COOKING
Seafood and Poultry
with WINE

© 2002 **Bruce Carlson**

. . . . dedicated to Maddie

4

SCALLOPS IN SAUCE

Handle scallops with care, because they are quite delicate and require only the briefest of cooking. Cook them too long and they become tough. With this recipe you may prepare the sauce, add the scallops and refrigerate the mixture until close to serving time. Allow time for a brief and careful reheating and an interval under the broiler.

¾ cup Dry Sauterne
1½ pounds frozen scallops, thawed and drained

3 tablespoons butter or margarine
3 green onions, chopped
¾ cup canned drained mushrooms
1 tablespoon chopped parsley
Dash each of salt, pepper, marjoram, thyme
1½ tablespoons flour
¾ cup undiluted evaporated milk
Paprika, bread crumbs, butter

In medium saucepan heat wine; add scallops and simmer for about 3 minutes, or until done. Drain cooked scallops (saving liquid) and keep scallops warm. In another saucepan melt butter; add onions and cook until barely tender. Add mushrooms, parsley, salt, pepper, marjoram and thyme. Remove from heat; blend in flour gradually, keeping smooth. Slowly stir in evaporated milk and ½ cup liquid from scallops; heat to boiling, stirring constantly. (Sauce should be thick.) Add paprika and scallops; remove from heat. Fill individual baking dishes with mixture. Sprinkle with bread crumbs then dot with butter. Place under broiler until slightly browned. Serve immediately.

10

PRAWNS SARAPICO

There will be a surprise package for each guest when you serve prawns this way. The prawns are cooked in individual squares of aluminum foil. Two kinds of cheese and pimientos with a generous portion of Chablis form an interesting and quite good sauce. Serve the prawns with fluffy cooked rice.

    1½ **pounds fresh or frozen prawns, uncooked**
    2 **(3-oz.) packages cream cheese**
    2 **(3-oz.) packages bleu cheese**

2 pimientos, chopped fine
8 thin slices lemon
½ cup Chablis

Shell and clean prawns. Cream together cheeses and pimientos. Cut four squares of aluminum foil. On

each square, mound an equal amount of cheese mixture. Flatten cheese mounds slightly with back of spoon. Divide raw prawns, placing equal amounts on each mound. Top each with two lemon slices. Bring edges of foil up to form a bag. Place bags on baking sheet. Just before sealing bags, pour 2 tablespoons Chablis in each. Bake in moderate oven (350°) 20 to 25 minutes or until prawns are done. Serve with fluffy cooked rice.

HALIBUT FLORENTINE

- 1½ pounds halibut steak
- ½ cup Medium Sauterne
- ½ cup lemon juice
- 1 (10-oz.) package frozen chopped spinach
- ¼ cup finely chopped onion
- 2 tablespoons butter or margarine
- 3 tablespoons flour
- ¼ teaspoon salt
  Dash pepper
- 1 cup undiluted evaporated milk
- 4 egg yolks, beaten
- ½ cup shredded Cheddar cheese

Place halibut in shallow skillet; add wine and lemon juice, then enough water to just cover fish; cover pan partially, bring to boil and simmer gently about 5 to 7 minutes. (Be careful not to over-cook.) With wide server, remove fish to lightly buttered shallow baking dish or casserole. Boil down liquid to about ¾ cup. In another saucepan cook spinach and onions in ¼ cup water with ½ teaspoon salt according to package directions; drain. Push spinach to one side of pan, add butter, stirring to melt, then blend in flour, salt, and pepper; cook briefly. Pour in evaporated milk and the ¾ cup liquid from fish. Cook and stir over medium heat until sauce thickens and all ingredients are combined. Remove from heat and spoon a small portion into egg yolks; return to sauce pan and stir to blend well. Pour over poached halibut in baking dish. Top with shredded cheese. Bake in hot oven (400°) about 10 minutes until cheese is melted and dish is well heated. Serve at once.

SCAMPI

Shrimp prepared in this way may be used as a light main course, serving toast squares or rice with it. Or the shrimp are delightful as hot hors d'oeuvres when offered in a chafing dish. The amount in each 5-ounce can is about 1 cup, so if you wish to use frozen or fresh-cooked shelled shrimp in this recipe, you will need about 2 cups.

    2 (5-oz.) cans shrimp, drained
    ¼ cup butter or margarine

⅛ teaspoon garlic chips
2 tablespoons parsley flakes
½ cup Chablis or other white table wine

Melt butter or margarine in skillet or chafing dish. Add garlic, parsley and wine. Heat to simmering then add shrimp and cook over low heat until heated through, about 5 minutes.

PEAS AT SEA

  1 (10-oz.) package little baby early peas
     frozen in butter sauce
  2 tablespoons all-purpose flour
  1 cup milk
  1 cup grated Cheddar cheese
  3 tablespoons Dry Sherry
 ⅛ teaspoon white pepper
  2 (6½-oz.) cans crabmeat, drained and flaked
  1 (4½-oz.) can large shrimps, drained
  2 tablespoons butter or margarine, melted
 ⅓ cup fine bread crumbs
    Paprika

Slip pouch of peas into boiling water; bring water to second boil; continue cooking until butter sauce is melted. Open pouch; drain butter sauce into medium saucepan; stir in flour; gradually add milk. Place over medium heat; cook until thickened, stirring constantly. Add cheese; heat until melted. Stir in Sherry, pepper, crabmeat, shrimps and peas. Spoon into four large lightly greased baking shells; allow ¾ cup per serving. Combine butter and bread crumbs. Sprinkle around outside edge of baking shells. Bake in moderate oven (350°) 25 minutes. Dust with paprika before serving.

CLAM CASSEROLE

½ pound wide noodles
2 tablespoons butter or margarine
2 tablespoons salad oil
1 medium-sized onion, minced
1 clove garlic, minced
5 tablespoons flour
2 (7-oz.) cans minced clams
1 (No. 2) can stewed tomatoes
½ cup Sauterne or other white table wine
1 cup grated Cheddar cheese
½ teaspoon Worcestershire sauce
Salt and pepper to taste

Cook noodles in boiling salted water until tender; drain. Heat butter and oil in a heavy skillet or saucepan; add onion and garlic; cook gently, stirring frequently, for 5 minutes. Blend in flour; add liquid drained from clams, tomatoes and wine; cook, stirring constantly, until mixture boils and thickens. Add ½ cup of the cheese; stir over low heat until melted. Season with Worcestershire sauce, salt and pepper. Add clams and noodles. Turn into a greased casserole; sprinkle with remaining ½ cup grated cheese. Bake in a moderately hot oven (375°) 25 minutes.

BRAISED PRAWNS

  1 pound uncooked prawns, shelled and deveined
¼ cup cooking oil
  1 (5-oz.) can sliced bamboo shoots

¾ cup stock
¼ cup Dry Sherry
1 teaspoon soy sauce
1 teaspoon sugar
¼ cup finely chopped cooked ham
1 tablespoon vinegar
1 tablespoon cornstarch

Cut prawns in half lengthwise without cutting all the way through; press flat with wide knife. In large skillet, heat oil, add bamboo shoots and cook gently about 5 minutes. Add prawns, stock, wine, soy sauce and sugar, mixing well. Cook over medium heat 5 minutes; add ham and stir briefly. Spoon out into serving dish, leaving liquid in pan. Combine vinegar and cornstarch; gradually add to liquid stirring constantly until sauce thickens and clears. Pour over shrimp mixture. Serve with additional soy sauce or on hot cooked rice.

OYSTER STEW

White wine is very good in oyster stew. Heat 1½ cups milk with ½ cup light cream. Melt ¼ cup butter in skillet; add 1 pint oysters and their liquid. Cook just until edges of oysters start to curl. Add ¼ cup Chablis or other white table wine,
1 teaspoon seasoned salt and a dash of white pepper. Combine with the heated milk and serve.

POACHED FISH

1½ pounds fish fillets or steaks
1 small onion, minced
2 sprigs parsley
1 tablespoon butter or margarine
¾ cup Chablis or other white table wine
Salt and pepper
½ cup heavy cream
¼ cup grated Parmesan cheese

Place large sheet of heavy duty foil wrap on shallow baking pan. Sprinkle half of onion in center and arrange fish on it, overlapping fillets. If very thin fillets are used, roll them up jelly-roll fashion and fasten with picks. Sprinkle fish with remaining onion, add

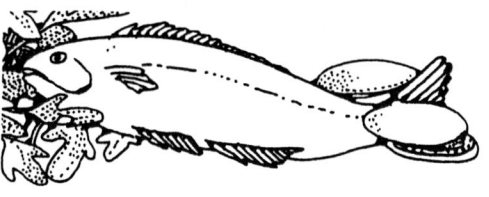

parsley sprigs and dot with butter. Pour wine over all; season with salt and pepper. Make cooking package by bringing long ends of foil up over fish and sealing with double fold; fold and turn up ends of foil to hold in juices. Bake in moderate oven (375°) 20 minutes. Gently pour out liquid in package into measuring cup. (There should be slightly more than 1 cupful.) Place package with fish on heat proof platter or serving dish; or remove fillets carefully from foil and arrange on platter.

Make sauce: In saucepan melt 3 tablespoons butter
or margarine and blend in 3 tablespoons flour; cook

and stir well, then add hot fish liquid gradually, stirring vigorously to smooth. Add cream, using just enough to make a sauce of medium consistency. Taste for seasoning content. You may want to add a few drops of lemon juice and salt. Open foil and crimp to form border. Pour sauce over fish; sprinkle with Parmesan cheese, then brown under broiler.

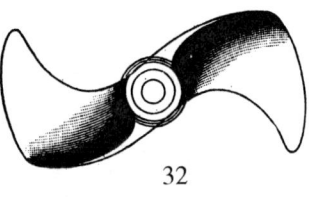

BAKED FISH FILLETS

- ½ cup Sauterne or other white table wine
- ¼ cup white wine vinegar
- ¼ cup water
- 1 teaspoon salt
- 1 pound fish fillets (sole, halibut or cod)
  Fine dry bread crumbs
- ½ cup mayonnaise
- ½ cup dairy sour cream
- 2 tablespoons finely chopped green onion
  Paprika

33

Combine wine, vinegar, water and salt; pour over fish fillets and marinate 1 to 2 hours. Drain fish thoroughly on paper toweling. Coat both sides of fillets with crumbs; arrange in single layer in lightly buttered shallow baking dish. Combine mayonnaise, sour cream and onion; spread evenly over fish. Cover with thin layer of crumbs and dust with paprika. Bake in a hot oven (425°) for 10 minutes, or until fish is done. Serve with lemon wedges.

TUNA CASSEROLE

- 1 (3-oz.) can chow mein noodles
- 1 (10½-oz.) can condensed cream of mushroom soup
- 1 (7-oz.) can tuna
- ¼ cup Chablis or other white table wine
- 1 cup thinly sliced celery
- 1 tablespoon instant minced onion
- Pepper

Set aside ½ cup noodles for topping. Blend all other ingredients and place in lightly greased casserole; sprinkle with reserved noodles. Bake in moderate oven (350°) about 30 to 40 minutes.

SHRIMP NEWBURG

    1 (10-oz.) can frozen cream of shrimp soup, thawed
¼ cup evaporated milk
    1 (5-oz.) can deveined shrimp, well drained
    1 cup frozen peas, thawed
    1 cup shredded process American cheese
    2 tablespoons Dry Sherry
    1 teaspoon Worcestershire sauce
¼ teaspoon Tabasco

In saucepan combine soup and evaporated milk; heat gently. Stir in shrimp, peas, cheese, Sherry, Worcestershire sauce and Tabasco. Continue to cook over medium heat, stirring occasionally, until steaming. Do not boil. Serve over hot rice.

CIOPPINO ON THE EASY

  ¼ cup olive oil
  1 medium onion, finely chopped
  2 cloves garlic, crushed
  1 (1-lb. 12-oz.) can tomatoes
  2 (8-oz.) cans tomato sauce
  2 (1½-oz.) packages spaghetti-sauce-mix
  1 teaspoon seasoned salt
  ¼ teaspoon seasoned pepper
  2 cups water

      1 cup Dry Sauterne or other white table wine
  1½ pounds white fish, such as halibut,
           cut in large chunks
      1 pound raw shrimp or small prawns,
           shelled and deveined
      4 (about 6-oz.) uncooked lobster tails, fins and
           soft undershell removed and cut in large chunks,
           shell and all
      1 dozen well-washed clams

In large Dutch oven or kettle heat oil; add onion
and garlic and sauté until tender. Add tomatoes, tomato sauce, spaghetti-sauce-mix, seasoned salt, seasoned pepper and water. Bring to boil, reduce heat,
and simmer for 30 minutes, stirring occasionally.

Add wine, fish, shrimp, lobster and clams. Cover and simmer about 15 minutes, stirring occasionally. Serve in large soup bowls with chunks of heated French bread.

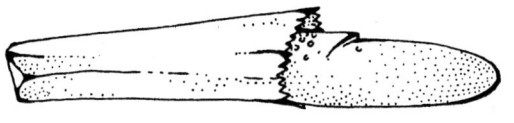

SALMON STEAKS

Dry Vermouth makes an effective marinade for seafood because of the many herbs and spices that go into its production. Use a glass or enamelware dish for the marinating, so there'll be no

chance of a metallic taste. While the salmon is on the grill, heat the seasoned wine mixture in which it is marinated, to use as a basting sauce.

- 2 pounds salmon steaks or other fish steaks, fresh or frozen
- 1 cup Dry Vermouth
- ¾ cup melted fat or oil
- ⅓ cup lemon juice
- 2 tablespoon chopped chives, fresh or freeze-dried
- 2 teaspoons seasoned salt
- ½ teaspoon seasoned pepper

Thaw frozen steaks. Cut into serving-size portions and place in single layer in shallow baking dish. Combine remaining ingredients. Pour sauce over fish and let stand 4 hours, turning occasionally. Remove fish, reserving sauce for basting. Place fish in well-greased, hinged wire grills. Cook about 4 inches from moderately hot coals 8 minutes. Baste with sauce. Turn and cook 7 to 10 minutes longer or until fish flakes easily when tested with a fork.

STEAK 'N SAUCE

1 (10½-oz.) can condensed tomato soup
⅓ cup Burgundy or other red table wine
1 cup shredded process pimiento cheese
2 tablespoons chopped parsley
1 tablespoon minced onion
4 fish steaks (halibut, swordfish, sea bass, salmon)

In saucepan combine soup, wine and cheese; stir over low heat until cheese melts. Add parsley and onion. Arrange fish steaks in shallow baking dish; pour hot wine sauce over them. Bake in moderate oven (375°) 25 to 30 minutes.

SHRIMP 'N TUNA

   1 (10½-oz.) can condensed cream of celery soup
   ½ cup mayonnaise
   ½ cup diced celery
   ½ cup sliced ripe olives
   ¼ cup chopped onion
   1 (7-oz.) can tuna
   2 tablespoons Dry Sherry
   1 (5-oz.) can shrimp
   6 pastry shells, heated until crisp

In a saucepan combine soup, mayonnaise, celery, olives and onion. Place over heat, add Sherry and oil drained from tuna, stirring well to smooth. Add tuna broken into pieces and drained shrimp, combining gently. Continue cooking gently until well heated. Serve in pastry shells.

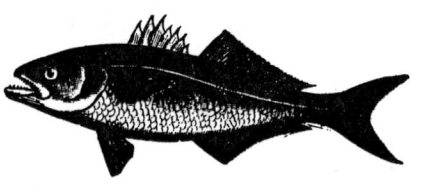

FISH AND TOMATO

1 (3- to 4-lb.) fish for baking
2 tablespoons lemon juice
  Salt and pepper
1 cup chopped onions
½ cup finely chopped parsley
2 small cloves garlic, minced
¼ cup cooking oil
½ cup Dry Sauterne
1 cup tomato catsup
1 cup tomato juice

Rinse fish in cold water; dry well. Rub with lemon juice and sprinkle inside and out with salt and pepper; place in baking dish. In skillet sauté onions, parsley, and garlic in oil until onions are transparent, but not browned. Stir in Sauterne and remaining ingredients; simmer about 5 minutes, then pour over fish. Bake uncovered in moderate oven (350°), basting occasionally, allowing about 16 minutes per pound. Serve garnished with sliced lemon wheels and parsley.

SHRIMP NEWBURG

If time is limited, the Sherry-flavored sauce for this shrimp may be made in advance and refrigerated until just before serving time. Reheat the sauce in the top of a double boiler over hot water, adding the shrimp at the very last. Thin the sauce to desired consistency with a small portion of the Sherry marinade.

½ cup Dry Sherry
2 cups cooked and cleaned shrimp
3 tablespoons butter or margarine
2 tablespoons all-purpose flour
¾ cup light or heavy cream
Yolks of 4 hard-cooked eggs
1 teaspoon salt
¼ teaspoon dry mustard
Dash of pepper
2 tablespoons lemon juice
4 cups hot cooked rice

Pour Sherry over shrimp. Cover and marinate several hours. Drain and reserve ¼ cup liquid. Combine butter and flour in top of double boiler. Add cream and cook, stirring constantly, until sauce thickens and smooths; do not boil. Press egg yolks through sieve into bowl. Rub to paste and stir, a little at a time, into hot sauce. Stir until smooth. Add ¼ cup Sherry marinade, salt, dry mustard, pepper, and lemon juice. When ready to serve, stir in shrimp. Some of the remaining marinade may be added for extra flavor and to thin sauce if necessary. Heat through. Serve over hot, cooked rice or individual rice rings.

Individual Rice Rings: Add 3 tablespoons butter or margarine to hot rice. Pack into 4 greased individual ring molds. Set in pan of hot water for about 1 minute, then invert on serving plates.

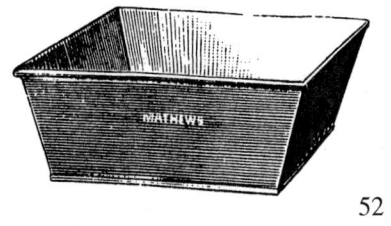

POULTRY

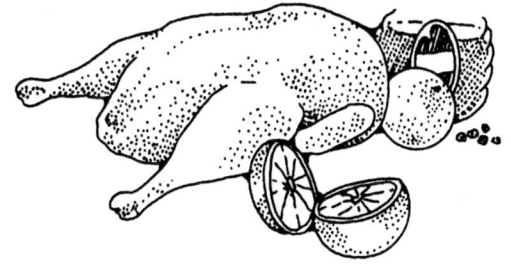

CORNISH HEN

2 (1-lb., 6-oz.) Cornish hens
1 cup Dry Sauterne or other white table wine
1 tablespoon salad oil
1 (7-oz.) package herb stuffing mix
  Salt and pepper
1 cup dairy sour cream
¼ cup melted butter or margarine

Defrost Cornish hens; remove giblets; cut each hen in half. Wipe dry, then marinate several hours in wine and oil. Crush 2 cups of the dressing mix into very fine crumbs. Drain hens well; sprinkle with salt and pepper; spread with sour cream. Coat thickly with fine dressing mix crumbs. Combine remaining dressing mix with wine and oil in which hens were marinated; add 2 tablespoons of the melted butter. Spread in shallow baking pan. Place coated hens over dressing mix; drizzle with remaining melted butter. Bake in a moderate oven (350°) about 1 hour or until tender.

CHICKEN BREASTS IN SOUR CREAM

4 small chicken breasts
2 teaspoons salt
1 teaspoon pepper
¼ cup butter, and 2 tablespoons butter
½ cup Dry Sauterne or other white table wine
⅓ cup finely chopped onion
1 cup dairy sour cream
¼ cup sliced pitted ripe olives
¼ cup chopped fresh chives

Remove skin from chicken breasts; sprinkle chicken with salt and pepper. Melt 1/4 cup butter in skillet. Add chicken and sauté carefully until golden, turning occasionally. Pour wine over chicken, cover and steam until tender, 20 to 25 minutes. Remove chicken breasts to heated serving platter and place in warm oven. Add 2 tablespoons butter and onions to skillet; sauté until soft, then stir in sour cream and olives. Heat gently but do not boil. Add chives and pour over chicken. Serve with rice or small new potatoes and peas.

SHERRIED CHICKEN

1 package noodles romanoff
1 (10½-oz.) can condensed cream of mushroom soup
2 (5-oz.) cans boned chicken, drained, or
   2 cups cooked chicken, coarsely diced
1 (10-oz.) package frozen chopped broccoli,
   thawed and well drained
½ cup pitted ripe olives, cut into wedges
¼ cup Dry Sherry

Prepare noodles romanoff as directed on package except increase milk to ¾ cup. Stir in remaining ingredients; pour into 2-quart casserole. Cover and bake in moderate oven (350°) 25 to 30 minutes or until broccoli is tender.

SEAGOING CHICKEN

    ¼ cup butter or margarine
    ¼ cup finely minced onion
    ¼ cup all-purpose flour
    1¼ cups milk
    ½ cup light cream
    2 chicken bouillon cubes
    1½ cups cubed, cooked chicken
    ¾ cup cubed, canned lobster
    ½ cup sliced canned mushrooms

½ cup **Medium Sherry**
   Salt and pepper to taste
1 **egg yolk, slightly beaten**

In saucepan melt butter, add onion and cook until transparent but not brown. Blend in flour then add milk, cream and bouillon cubes, stirring constantly; cook until smooth and thickened. Add chicken, lobster and mushrooms; heat to serving temperature. Add wine, salt and pepper to taste, and egg yolk. Cook over low heat, stirring gently until sauce is thickened.

CHICKEN WITH SAUTERNE

1 (2½-lb.) broiler-fryer, cut up
1 teaspoon seasoned salt
1 package spaghetti sauce mix
½ cup fine dry bread crumbs
¼ cup salad oil
½ cup Dry Sauterne
3 fresh tomatoes, peeled and quartered
2 cups sliced fresh mushrooms

Sprinkle chicken pieces with seasoned salt. Blend dry spaghetti sauce mix with crumbs; coat chicken pieces. In heavy skillet sauté chicken carefully in heated oil. Add wine, tomatoes, mushrooms and remaining crumb mixture. Cover and simmer over low heat, about 45 minutes or until chicken is tender.

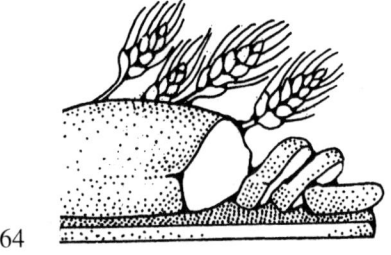

CHICKEN LIVERS SAUTE'

¼ cup butter or margarine
1 pound chicken livers, fresh or frozen, cut up
3 tablespoons flour
1 cup canned consomme or bouillon-cube broth
½ cup Dry Sherry
  Salt and pepper
1 (3-oz.) can sliced, broiled mushrooms, drained
2 tablespoons chopped parsley

Heat butter in skillet; add livers and sauté quickly until well browned, turning frequently; remove from pan to warm plate and add flour to pan drippings and blend well; add consomme and Sherry; cook, stirring constantly, until mixture is thickened and smooth; season. Add livers, mushrooms and parsley to sauce. Heat and serve on toast or with rice.

CHICKEN ON RICE

1 tablespoon butter or margarine
2 tablespoons flour
1 cup chicken broth
3 cups cooked chicken, in large pieces
¼ cup diced cooked ham
1 teaspoon salt
⅛ teaspoon pepper
2 tablespoons chopped pimiento
1 egg, slightly beaten
1 cup dairy sour cream

¼ cup Dry Sauterne or other white table wine
½ cup diced Swiss cheese
3 cups hot fluffy rice

In saucepan melt butter, blend in flour; add broth and cook, stirring constantly until thick and smooth. Add chicken, ham, salt, pepper, and pimiento; heat thoroughly. Stir together beaten egg, sour cream and wine, then add to sauce; add cheese and cook only until cheese melts. Serve over hot rice.

CHICKEN TETRAZZINI

    4 ounces spaghetti, broken
    1 (10½-oz.) can condensed cream of chicken soup
    1 (4-oz.) can sliced mushrooms
    1 small onion, chopped
 ¼ cup diced pimiento
 ¼ cup diced green pepper
1¾ cups grated sharp Cheddar cheese
    2 (5-oz.) cans boned chicken, cut up
 ¼ cup Sauterne or other white table wine

Cook spaghetti following package directions; drain.

Mix soup, mushrooms and liquid, chopped onion, pimiento, green pepper and 1¼ cups of the cheese. Add spaghetti, chicken and broth and Sauterne; toss lightly until mixed. Put in casserole and sprinkle with remaining cheese. Cover; bake in moderate oven (375°) 15 minutes; uncover and continue baking an additional 30 minutes.

STUFFED CHICKEN

        2 teaspoons grated lemon peel
        1 teaspoon grated orange peel
      ⅓ cup orange juice
        2 tablespoons lemon juice
      ½ cup brown sugar, firmly packed
      ¼ cup Dry Sherry
   1½ quarts (½-inch) soft bread cubes
      ⅔ cup chopped parsley
        1 teaspoon salt
        1 (3-lb.) frying chicken, quartered

In small saucepan place 1 teaspoon of the lemon peel, all of the orange peel, orange and lemon juices and brown sugar; bring to boil and simmer 20 minutes. Remove from heat and add Sherry. Combine soft bread cubes, parsley, salt and remaining lemon peel. Place bread mixture in bottom of lightly greased (9-inch) square baking dish. Top with chicken. Pour half of the sauce over chicken and bake in moderate oven (350°) 45 minutes. Pour remaining sauce over chicken and cook for an additional 30 minutes.

CHICKEN WITH SHERRY

  1 (3½-lb.) frying chicken, cut in serving pieces
  2 tablespoon all-purpose flour
  ½ teaspoon each salt, pepper
  2 tablespoons olive or salad oil
  1 (8-oz.) can tomato sauce
  1 cup stock or bouillon
  ½ cup Dry Sherry
  1 cup sliced mushrooms
  ½ cup sliced pimiento-stuffed olives

Coat chicken pieces well with combined flour, salt

and pepper; sauté in heated oil until lightly browned. Add remaining ingredients; cover pan and cook over low heat about 50 to 60 minutes, or until chicken is tender, lifting chicken pieces occasionally. Serve with hot fluffy rice.

CHICKEN IN FOIL

    1 onion, chopped
    1 stalk celery with leaves, chopped
    2 broiler chickens, quartered
    3 tablespoons olive oil
    1 (8½-oz.) can garbanzo beans or chick peas
    1 teaspoon salt
      Freshly ground black pepper
  ½ teaspoon oregano
    1 (8-oz.) can tomato sauce
  ½ cup Burgundy

Place large sheet of heavy duty foil wrap on shallow pan. Add onion and celery and then the chicken, cut side up. Brush chicken with olive oil. Brown lightly under broiler, turning chicken once and again brushing with oil. Add garbanzo beans and seasonings. Blend together tomato sauce and wine; pour over chicken. Close foil to make a tight package. Return to oven and bake in moderate oven (350°) about 1½ hours. Serve from the foil with crusty Italian bread and tossed green salad.

CHICKEN ON THE EASY

Here's the easiest way possible to make "company chicken." Arrange halved chickens (allowing one half per serving) in baking pan. Dot with butter, sprinkle with salt and dried herbs, and add about ½ cup white table wine.
Cover and bake in moderate oven about one hour, basting occasionally. Uncover and bake about 15 minutes longer, until tender and browned. Make

gravy from the rich drippings to serve over almond-rice.

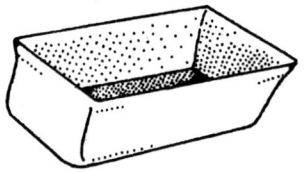

CHICKEN 'N CHILI

1 (5-lb.) stewing chicken
2 cups Chablis or other
  white table wine
2 cups water
3 teaspoons salt
1½ cups canned tomato puree
1 cup dairy sour cream
½ teaspoon finely chopped canned green chili
1 (6½-oz.) bag corn chips
½ cup pitted ripe olives, whole or halved
1 cup grated Cheddar cheese

Have chicken cut in serving pieces. Place in large kettle. Add wine, water, 2 teaspoons salt; cover and simmer until meat is fork tender, about 1½ hours. Cool chicken in broth, then remove and discard bones and skin. Keep chicken in large pieces when possible. Blend tomato puree, sour cream, chili powder, green chili and remaining 1 teaspoon salt together. Crush corn chips coarsely. Layer chicken, sauce, corn chips, olives and cheese in large casserole (about 1½ quart size). Bake in a moderate oven (350°) until hot and bubbly, 30 to 40 minutes.

TURKEY WITH STUFFING

2 cups cubed cooked turkey
3 cups (¼-inch) bread cubes
½ cup melted butter or margarine
2 tablespoons finely chopped onion
½ teaspoon each poultry seasoning, salt
¼ teaspoon pepper
2 tablespoons flour
1½ cups turkey or chicken stock
½ cup Dry Sherry

Combine turkey, bread cubes, 6 tablespoons of the butter, onion and seasonings; arrange in lightly greased 1-quart casserole. Melt remaining 2 tablespoons butter and blend in flour; add turkey stock and Sherry and cook, stirring constantly, until sauce boils and thickens. Pour over ingredients in casserole. Bake in moderate oven (350°) about 35 minutes.

WINE BAKED CHICKEN

    1 (2-lb.) broiler-fryer chicken, quartered
    1 teaspoon monosodium glutamate
   ¼ cup Medium Sauterne
    1 tablespoon melted butter or margarine
    1 teaspoon salt
   ⅛ teaspoon pepper
    1 teaspoon minced tarragon

Dry chicken pieces well with paper toweling. Sprinkle with monosodium glutamate; place, skin side up, in shallow baking pan. Combine wine, butter, salt, pepper and tarragon. Spoon wine mixture evenly over chicken. Bake in moderate oven (375°) about 45 to 50 minutes, or until tender, basting every fifteen minutes with pan juices.

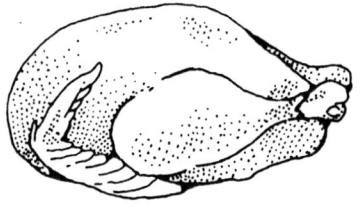

GRILLED TURKEY HALVES

2 (4- to 5-lb.) young turkeys
1 cup Dry Sauterne or Sherry
1 tablespoon seasoned herb mix
1 teaspoon each salt, hickory-smoked salt
2 tablespoons each tomato catsup, oil, brown sugar, garlic flavored red wine vinegar

Lay turkey halves in flat shallow pan. Combine all remaining ingredients. Pour over turkey, cover and marinate for several hours, turning turkey occasionally. When ready to cook, lift turkey from marinade and place breast side down over glowing coals on grill. Turkey should be about 9 inches from the heat. Grill 40 to 45 minutes, basting now and then with marinade; turn turkey halves. Make a hood of heavy duty quilted foil to cover turkey, lay loosely over meat on grill. Continue cooking until turkey is tender, about 30 to 40 minutes longer, or until drumstick twists easily in thigh joint.

TURKEY SANDWICHES

1 (2-lb.) package giblet gravy and sliced turkey
½ cup Chablis
1 loaf brown-and-serve French bread
3 tablespoons butter or margarine, softened
⅛ teaspoon crushed thyme
1 (3½-oz.) can French-fried onion rings

Heat turkey according to package directions; carefully remove slices. Pour gravy into skillet, add wine and boil until reduced to almost half amount (about 1½ cups). Add sliced turkey. Meanwhile, split

French bread and bake according to package directions. Combine butter and thyme, spread on bread, and cut each half into three pieces. Place heated slices of turkey on bread; spoon on gravy. Sprinkle slightly heated onion rings on top.

TURKEY WITH SHERRY

2 tablespoons Medium Sherry
1 (10½-oz.) can condensed cream of mushroom soup
2 cups finely diced cooked turkey
2 cups baked stuffing
2 eggs, slightly beaten

Combine Sherry and soup for sauce. Combine turkey, stuffing and eggs with ½ cup of the sauce, mixing well. Place ½ cup of the turkey mixture into each of 6 well-greased custard cups; set in shallow pan of water and bake in moderate oven (350°) about 40 minutes or until firm. Unmold and serve with remainder of Sherry Mushroom sauce, heated.

TURKEY WITH WINE SAUCE

For a quick and easy way to roast turkey, start with one of the prepared (about 2½ lbs.) turkey roasts and follow the directions given on the package. When the roast is cooked, remove it from the foil roasting pan and add to the drippings: 1 tablespoon finely chopped onion, ¼ cup Sauterne or other dry white table wine, ¼ cup tomato sauce, ⅓ cup water and ½ the contents of a gravy packet. Heat mixture to boiling point, stirring to blend well. Serve over slices of roast turkey.

ROAST WILD DUCK

2 (1-lb.) wild ducks
1 package French salad dressing mix
6 celery stalks and leaves
2 tablespoons melted butter or salad oil
⅓ cup diced onion (optional)
½ teaspoon coarsely ground black pepper
¼ cup diced orange
1 cup Burgundy

Clean and wash ducks thoroughly; singe and wash again. Dry well. Rub inside and out with dry salad dressing mix. Stuff celery stalks into body cavities. Place ducks in roasting pan; brush with butter. Roast in hot oven (400°) about 10 minutes or until lightly browned, turning once. Pour off excess fat. Turn ducks breast side up and cover with onion, pepper, orange, and wine. Return to oven and roast 20 minutes longer for very rare; 40 minutes for medium; and 1 hour and 5 minutes for well-done. Remove celery stalks before serving.

PHEASANT IN SAUCE

½ cup all-purpose flour
1 teaspoon each salt, paprika
⅛ teaspoon each pepper, powdered sweet basil
2 pheasants, cut into pieces
¼ cup shortening
1 small clove garlic, crushed
½ cup water
½ teaspoon Worcestershire sauce
¼ cup chopped ripe olives
½ cup Chablis or other white table wine

Combine flour, salt, paprika, pepper and basil; coat pheasant pieces well. Brown on all sides in shortening in large skillet. Add garlic, water and Worcestershire sauce. Cover pan tightly and simmer 45 minutes. Turn pheasant and add olives and wine. Recover pan and simmer 35 to 45 minutes longer or until tender. Add additional wine if necessary to increase amount of sauce.

TURKEY WITH WAFFLES

 ¼ cup butter or margarine
 ½ cup all-purpose flour
  1 tablespoon chicken seasoned stock base
 ¼ teaspoon each white pepper, dry mustard
 ⅛ teaspoon nutmeg
2¾ cups milk
  2 to 4 tablespoons Dry Sherry
  2 cups cubed cooked turkey

In saucepan melt butter and blend in flour, chicken base, pepper, mustard and nutmeg. Add milk gradually and cook over medium heat, stirring constantly until sauce thickens, about 8 minutes. Stir in Sherry and turkey; cook until turkey is well heated through. Serve over Herb Waffles. To make the Herb Waffles, add 1 teaspoon poultry seasoning to each cup of waffle mix.

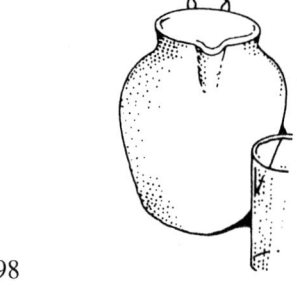

CREAMED CHICKEN

       6 tablespoons butter or margarine
     ½ cup all-purpose flour
       1 teaspoon salt
       1 (10½-oz.) can condensed chicken broth
    1⅔ cups milk
       1 cup diced cooked mushrooms (optional)
       2 cups diced cooked chicken
     ¼ cup Dry Sherry
       2 cups corn chips

In saucepan melt butter and blend in flour and salt;

add broth and milk gradually. Cook about 8 minutes, stirring constantly. Add mushrooms and chicken; heat thoroughly, then add Sherry. Serve on corn chips.

HOT CHICKEN

You'll have to try this unorthodox method of cooking beautifully browned chicken to be convinced.

The secret is in using Cream Sherry, which is sweet enough to help brown and glaze the chicken, and a high temperature not usually associated with chicken cookery.

6 large pieces frying chicken
  Salt and pepper
½ cup butter
1 cup Cream Sherry

Season chicken with salt and pepper; sprinkle, if desired, lightly with your favorite herb. Place chicken pieces close together and skin-side down in baking pan. Slice butter over chicken; pour on Cream

Sherry. Bake in hot oven (425°) 15 minutes. Turn chicken pieces, skin-side up. Continue baking until tender, 40 to 45 minutes longer.

DELLA ROBIA CHICKEN

The inspiration for garnishing a roast chicken or turkey with a ring of wine-spiced fruits comes from the Della Robia plaques and platters of Italy.

1 (5-lb.) roasting chicken
Salt and Pepper
¼ cup melted butter or shortening

Season chicken, inside and out, with salt and pepper. Place in pan, brush on melted shortening. Bake in hot oven (450°) for 15 minutes, just until chicken begins to take on color. Reduce heat to moderate (350°) and roast, uncovered, ½ hour. Spoon one quarter of Wine Baste (below) over chicken and continue roasting for about one hour longer, basting frequently with additional Wine Baste.

Wine Baste   (Makes about 2 cups)

- 1 cup Rosé or Chablis or other white table wine
- ¼ cup wine vinegar
- ⅔ cup cooking oil
- 1 teaspoon dry mustard

1 tablespoon seasoned salt
1 teaspoon seasoned pepper
½ teaspoon finely crumbled dried rosemary or oregano
¼ cup honey or brown sugar
2 teaspoons grated onion
1 small clove garlic, finely crushed

Combine all ingredients; heat to blend flavors, bring only to boiling. Cool. Brush over chicken frequently during roasting or grilling.

CHICKEN AND RIESLING

Carefully made, this chicken recipe will produce elegant results. The chicken must be nicely browned

and the vegetables cut evenly. Avoid over-cooking or handling so that each piece retains its shape in the very good sauce. The blazing of the chicken with brandy is optional, although it does add to the flavor of the dish. Warm the brandy in top of small double boiler over hot water, pour over the chicken and light. Spoon it up and over the pieces, and when the flames burn out, add the seasonings and proceed.

1 (2½- to 3-lb.) frying chicken, cut in quarters
½ cup all-purpose flour
¼ cup cooking oil
8 small white onions
4 carrots, cut in thirds, crosswise
4 shallots or scallions, finely chopped
¼ cup Brandy
¼ cup chopped parsley
1 teaspoon salt
½ teaspoon pepper
1 clove garlic
½ cup Riesling or other white table wine
½ pound mushroom caps

Dust chicken well with flour. In large heavy skillet heat oil and brown chicken lightly. Remove chicken and keep warm. To skillet add onions, carrots, and shallots; brown very lightly. Return chicken pieces and blaze with warmed brandy. Season with parsley, salt, pepper and garlic. Add Riesling, cover pan and simmer 25 minutes. Add mushrooms and turn chicken pieces. Continue cooking gently until chicken is tender, about 20 minutes. Remove garlic. Serve chicken and its sauce with baked potatoes.

CHICKEN & MUSHROOMS

    8 pieces frying chicken (breasts, thighs, legs)
    6 tablespoons butter or margarine
  ½ pound fresh mushrooms
       Salt, pepper
    1 tablespoon chopped parsley
    1 teaspoon rosemary
  ½ cup Dry Sherry or Sauterne

In heavy skillet, brown chicken lightly in butter or margarine. Have ready 4 large pieces of foil wrap and place 2 pieces of chicken in center of each. In the same skillet give the lightest touch of brown to the mushrooms; divide among the four servings. Sprinkle each serving with salt, pepper, parsley and rosemary. Add 2 tablespoons of wine to each. Bring ends of foil wrap together over chicken and seal in double fold; seal opposite ends to make tight package. Place packages in shallow pan and bake in moderate oven (375°) 1 hour. If serving very informally, open packages and crimp foil back around edges before placing on plate. Otherwise, transfer contents of package onto serving plate to accompany steamed rice or cooked noodles with parsley.

BBQ CHICKEN LEGS

8 chicken legs, both joints
1 (6-oz.) can tomato paste
½ cup tomato catsup
¼ cup brown sugar, firmly packed
½ cup Dry or Medium Sauterne
1 tablespoon each vinegar, soy sauce,
  prepared mustard, onion juice
2 teaspoons all-purpose seasoning
1 teaspoon barbecue spice
  Dash garlic powder or garlic salt
¼ teaspoon each monosodium glutamate, black pepper
¼ cup melted butter or margarine

113

Dry chicken legs well. In saucepan, combine all remaining ingredients, mixing well; place over low heat and bring to boil; simmer about 5 minutes. Adjust grill 5 to 6 inches from hot coals. Brush chicken legs with baste and place skin side down on grill; brown on both sides, then begin basting with sauce. Continue cooking, basting and turning legs frequently, about 45 minutes or until done. Serve with a little of the heated baste. Accompany with corn on the cob or a good potato salad, made with white wine dressing, and a generous tray of assorted relishes.

PEAR GARNISH

Use these simple-to-make but attractive bright red pear halves as a garnish for the turkey platter or with chicken and dum-

plings. Spoon contents 1 (1-lb. 13-oz.) can pear halves into deep bowl; drop 2 lemon slices on top. Measure syrup from pears and add enough water to make 1½ cups; pour into small saucepan. Add ½ cup Burgundy and ½ teaspoon red food coloring. Heat to boiling, then pour over pears. Cool; refrigerate several hours or overnight until pears are well flavored with the wine and absorb the color.

SAUCE FOR CHICKEN

Keep this super-rich sauce suggestion handy for leftover chicken, or a hurry-up seafood or tuna dish.   Blend ¼ cup Sherry into undiluted canned cream of celery soup. Add a teaspoon instant minced onion and ½ cup mayonnaise. Fold in chicken or seafood and heat thoroughly. Serve in avocado half shells or over toast squares.

CHICKEN A LA CREME

   3 tablespoons butter or margarine
1½ cups thinly sliced onions
   2 large chicken breasts, each cut in half
  ¾ teaspoon salt
  ¼ teaspoon each white pepper, curry powder
   4 medium artichokes
   2 tablespoons lemon juice
  ¾ cup Riesling or other white table wine
   3 cups heavy cream
     Fresh parsley sprigs

In large skillet or Dutch oven, melt butter and stir in onions. Cover and cook over low heat 5 minutes or until onions are tender but not browned. Add chicken to skillet and turn to coat with butter. Cover and cook over low heat for 10 minutes. Sprinkle with seasonings.

Meanwhile wash artichokes; cut off stems and remove bottom leaves. Quarter artichokes and remove chokes (thistle portion); rub cut edges with lemon juice. Add to chicken in skillet. Pour in wine; boil rapidly until liquid has almost evaporated. Pour in

2¾ cups of the cream which has been brought to a boil. Cover and simmer gently 35 to 45 minutes or until chicken and artichokes are tender. Transfer chicken and artichokes to platter and keep warm. Remove skillet from heat; stir in 1 tablespoon lemon juice. Gradually beat remaining ¼ cup cream into sauce. Pour over chicken and artichokes. Garnish with parsley and serve with rice.

BREAST OF CHICKEN

All the delicious flavor and juices of the chicken will
be held in when the chicken is cooked in foil wrap.

    2 center slices ready-to-eat ham, cut ¼ inch thick
  ¼ cup butter or margarine
    3 whole chicken breasts, each cut in half
    1 (10½-oz.) can condensed cream of chicken soup,
      undiluted

2 stalks celery, chopped
1 teaspoon minced onion
½ cup Medium Sauterne or
other white table wine
½ cup light cream

Cut ham into 6 servings; sauté until lightly browned

in butter. Place each portion of ham in center of large square of foil wrap. In the same skillet sauté chicken breasts lightly; place one on each portion of ham. In saucepan heat soup, celery, onion, wine and cream. Spoon equal portions onto each serving, about ½ cup each. Bring edges of foil wrap over chicken, sealing first in double fold, then sealing each end to make a tight package. Place packages on shallow baking sheet; bake in moderate oven (350°) 1¼ hours.

GLAZED TURKEY

For a party or for a large family gathering this beautifully glazed turkey will do justice to your carefully planned menu. Roast the turkey with or without

dressing, but keep basting it occasionally with the special wine and fruit juice baste.

1 (15- to 18-lb.) turkey
¼ cup butter or margarine, melted
3 tablespoons lemon juice
  Salt and pepper
1 cup Rose
⅔ cup cranberry juice
⅓ cup pineapple juice
½ cup honey

Prepare turkey for roasting in your usual way. Combine melted butter and lemon juice; brush about half of it over turkey; sprinkle with salt and pepper.

126

Place turkey in roasting pan and start roasting in moderate oven (350°). Combine Rosé with remainder of butter and other ingredients and when turkey begins to color, begin spooning on wine baste, 3 or 4 tablespoons at a time. Continue basting and roasting until turkey is glazed and tender, using wine baste and rich pan drippings. (Allow about 18 minutes to the pound.) Remove turkey to platter while making gravy. Skim excess fat from pan liquid; thicken liquid as desired with cornstarch mixed with water. Cook about 5 minutes. Pour into heated sauce bowl and serve with turkey.

CHICKEN WITH AVOCADO

1 (about 2½ lbs.) frying chicken, cut up
2 tablespoons flour
1 teaspoon salt
¼ teaspoon pepper
3 tablespoons cooking oil
1 medium onion, minced
1 clove garlic, minced
1 small green pepper, chopped
2 pieces celery, chopped
⅛ teaspoon each ground comino, paprika
½ cup Dry Sherry

½ cup chicken broth
1 whole pimiento, chopped
¼ cup sliced blanched almonds
2 firm avocados, peeled and diced

Coat chicken pieces in mixture of flour, salt and pepper. In heavy skillet, brown chicken carefully in heated oil. Add onion, garlic, green pepper and celery; cover and let simmer about 5 minutes. Add comino, paprika, chicken broth and wine; cover again and let simmer about 30 to 35 minutes or until chicken is tender. Add pimiento, almonds and avocado, distributing them carefully to avoid breaking the chicken pieces; let simmer a minute or so more. Taste and check salt content, adding a little more if necessary. Serve with steamed rice and fresh broccoli or asparagus.

TURKEY A LA KING

Use the last bits of a roast turkey
in a wine-flavored turkey a la king. Add about ¼
cup or more of Sauterne or Chablis to
creamed turkey mixture. Spoon over toasted Eng-
lish muffins and top with sprinkling of grated cheese
and slivered almonds.

TURKEY ON A STICK

Something different to broil over the barbecue coals, or under your range broiler if you wish, are these turkey squares. Purchase halves, quarters or cut-up turkey pieces. Remove the bones and skin, but try to keep the turkey in large pieces so they are easy to thread on skewers.

5 to 6 pounds uncooked turkey
1 cup Dry or Medium Sauterne or
other white table wine
⅓ cup soy sauce
½ cup finely chopped onion
1 crushed clove garlic
1 tablespoon fresh lemon juice
¼ cup oil

Cut turkey into 1½-inch chunks. Combine marinade ingredients and pour over meat; let stand 1 to 2 hours. Drain well; thread meat on skewers. Broil over charcoal, browning lightly on all sides. Do not overcook. Vegetables such as whole mushrooms, small whole tomatoes with green pepper squares between, and whole parboiled onions may be broiled at the same time, skewering each vegetable separately. Serve with mounds of rice, either on skewers or gently pulled from skewers and arranged on platter or serving plates.

TURKEY 'N MUSHROOMS

   1 (4-oz.) can mushroom pieces and stems, drained
      (save liquid)
   6 tablespoons melted butter or margarine
  ¼ cup all-purpose flour
  ¼ teaspoon each salt, paprika
      Pinch ground thyme
      Dash cayenne pepper
1½ cups light cream
  ¼ cup Dry Sherry
   2 egg yolks, slightly beaten

2 cups cubed (½-inch) cooked turkey roast
¼ cup grated Parmesan cheese
Toast points

Cook mushrooms in butter until lightly browned; blend in flour and seasonings. Gradually add ⅓ cup

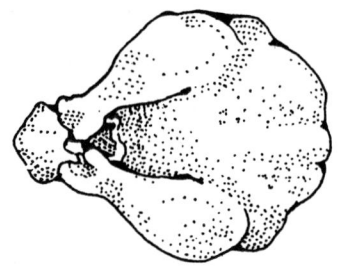

mushroom liquid and cream, stirring constantly until thickened. Stir in Sherry. Slowly add portion of hot sauce to egg yolks, stirring constantly, then stir egg mixture into remaining sauce. Place over low heat and cook until thick. Add turkey. Pour over toast points in 6 individual au gratin dishes; sprinkle with cheese and paprika. Place under broiler to brown slightly.

SHERRY CHICKEN

4 large boned chicken breasts, each cut in half
½ teaspoon seasoned pepper
1 teaspoon salt
2 tablespoons melted butter or margarine
3 slices bacon, diced
1 cup chopped onion
1 (4-oz.) can sliced mushrooms, undrained
2 tablespoons butter or margarine
3 tablespoons all-purpose flour
2¾ cups chicken broth
12 stuffed olives, sliced

½ cup Dry Sherry
4 cups cooked rice

Sprinkle chicken breasts with salt and pepper; brush with butter. Place in baking pan, cover and bake in a very hot oven (450°) 20 minutes; remove cover and continue cooking 20 minutes longer or until golden brown. Meanwhile prepare Sherry sauce: Sauté bacon and chopped onion until onion is tender; add sliced mushrooms, with liquid, and butter. Blend in flour; add broth gradually, stirring constantly to smooth. Add olives and Sherry, then simmer sauce over low heat 25 to 30 minutes.

CHICKEN CHABLIS

  1 (3½-lb.) chicken, cut in pieces
  ⅓ cup all-purpose flour
  1 teaspoon each salt, black pepper
  ½ cup butter or margarine
  ½ cup Chablis or other white table wine
  2 tablespoons instant minced onion
  ⅛ teaspoon ground nutmeg
  ½ teaspoon dry mustard
  2 teaspoons all-purpose seasoning
  1 tablespoon each celery flakes, sweet pepper flakes
  1 (4-oz.) can mushrooms
  1 (8-oz.) can tomato sauce
  1 cup water

Coat chicken pieces with mixture of flour, salt and pepper. Reserve leftover flour mixture. In heavy skillet, brown chicken in butter, then transfer to baking dish and pour wine over chicken. Blend reserved flour mixture into butter left in skillet; add remaining ingredients and simmer about 5 minutes; pour over chicken. Cover dish and bake in moderate oven (350°) 45 minutes or until tender. This is good to serve with hot cooked spaghetti.

ROAST DUCKLING

ALA ORANGE

1 (5- to 6-lb.) duckling, cut for fricassee
Salt

⅔ cup Port
1 tablespoon grated orange peel
1 clove garlic, minced
3 tablespoons cooking oil
1 tablespoon cornstarch
1¼ cups fresh orange juice
1 tablespoon honey
¼ teaspoon ground ginger
Dash pepper
1 cup fresh orange sections

With fork, puncture skin of duckling pieces; sprinkle with salt and place on rack in roasting pan; pour ½ cup of the Port over them. Roast in a slow oven (325°) basting and turning pieces occasionally, allowing about 25 minutes per pound. Keep warm while preparing sauce.

Orange Sauce: In saucepan, lightly sauté orange peel and garlic in cooking oil. Blend remaining Port with cornstarch, orange juice and honey; add slowly to saucepan, stirring constantly to smooth. Simmer sauce for a few minutes until clear, then stir in ginger, pepper and orange sections and heat well. Taste and add salt as necessary. Serve hot with roast duckling.

CHICKEN CURRY

In preparing this curry be sure to take into account the varied strength of curry powders and family preference. Start with a small amount of curry and gradually increase it to the desired proportion.

        2 (5-oz.) cans boned chicken
        1 (10½-oz.) can condensed cream of chicken soup
        1 teaspoon curry powder
        ¼ cup Sauterne or other white table wine
        3 cups hot steamed rice

Cut chicken into pieces. In skillet combine chicken with soup, curry powder and wine. Heat gently until well blended and hot. Serve over hot steamed rice. Offer a choice of condiments to sprinkle over curry, such as coconut, orange sections, chutney, chopped salted peanuts or crisp, crumbled bacon. Condiments may be in small bowls on one tray or in compartments of one large plate.

CHICKEN LIVERS AND BEEF TIPS

¼ cup butter
½ pound fresh
  mushrooms,
  cleaned and
  sliced
2 tablespoons
  butter

1 tablespoon
  flour
2 teaspoons
  paprika
1 teaspoon salt
⅛ teaspoon
  pepper

2 teaspoons finely chopped shallots or scallions

1 pound beef sirloin tips, cut in 3 by ½-inch strips

⅓ cup red wine vinegar

1 cup light cream

1 cup milk

2 egg yolks

1 pound chicken
   livers, cut into
   large pieces

In a skillet melt ¼ cup butter; sauté
mushrooms 2 to 3 minutes. Remove to
a warm plate. Melt additional 2 table-

spoons butter. Add shallots, beef, chicken livers; sprinkle with flour, paprika, salt and pepper and cook, stirring occasionally until browned. Add vinegar, bring to simmer and cook until most of liquid is reduced. Return mushrooms to pan. Combine cream and milk with lightly beaten egg yolk. Gradually add to hot mixture, cook a few minutes, stirring, until slightly thickened and hot. Transfer mixture to heated chafing dish for service. Serve piping hot over cooked noodles. Makes about 8 servings.

ROCK CORNISH GAME HENS

6 Rock Cornish
  hens
Salt
½ cup melted
  butter

2 cups dry white
  wine

Remove giblets from game hens. Wipe with a damp cloth. Sprinkle inside of

154

each hen with salt. Truss. Place hens in a shallow baking dish. Pour melted butter over hens. Roast in a very hot oven (450°F.) 20 minutes. Pour wine over hens. Reduce heat to moderate (350°F.) and continue roasting 35 to 40 minutes longer, or until birds are just tender. Baste frequently during cooking time

WINE-BASTED CORNISH HENS

2 (14 to 16 ounces)
  Rock Cornish
  hens
Celery
Onion
Seasoned salt
Pepper

⅓ cup butter
½ cup white
  dinner wine
⅓ cup orange
  juice
1 tablespoon
  lemon juice

156

Remove giblets from hens. Place giblets in a small pan with salted water, 1 stalk celery and ½ small onion. Simmer until tender. Sprinkle inside cavity of each hen with seasoned salt and pepper. Place a small piece of celery and onion inside each hen. Truss birds using wooden picks and tying legs together with string. Place in a shallow roasting pan. Melt butter and pour over birds. Sprinkle with seasoned salt and pepper. Roast in a very hot oven (450°F.) 20 minutes. Spoon on wine, orange and lemon juices. Continue roasting, basting often with pan sauce, until birds are tender and nicely browned, about 40 minutes longer. Remove birds to hot plate and keep warm. Skim off any excess fat from juices in pan. Stir ½ cup of the giblet broth into pan. Bring to boil loosening all brown particles. Taste and correct seasoning, if needed. Add chopped giblets. Spoon a little of the rich pan sauce over each hen when served. Makes 2 servings.

MY OWN FAVORITE

MY OWN FAVORITE

MY OWN FAVORITE

MY OWN FAVORITE

MY OWN FAVORITE

MY OWN FAVORITE

MY OWN FAVORITE

MY OWN FAVORITE

MY OWN FAVORITE

MY OWN FAVORITE

MY OWN FAVORITE

MY OWN FAVORITE

NEED GIFTS?

Are you up a stump for some nice gifts for some nice people in your life? Here's a list of some great cookbooks. Just check 'em off, stick a check in an envelope with this page, and we'll get your books off to you. Add $2.75 for shipping and handling for the first book and then $.50 cents more for each additional one. If you order over $50.00, forget the shipping and handling.

Mini Cookbooks
(Only 3 1/2 x 5) With Maxi Good Eatin' - 160 or 176 pages - $5.95

- ❑ Arizona Cooking
- ❑ Arkansas Cooking
- ❑ Dakota Cooking
- ❑ Illinois Cooking
- ❑ Indiana Cooking
- ❑ Iowa Cookin'
- ❑ Kansas Cookin'
- ❑ Kentucky Cookin'
- ❑ Michigan Cooking
- ❑ Minnesota Cookin'
- ❑ Missouri Cookin'
- ❑ New Jersey Cooking
- ❑ New Mexico Cooking
- ❑ New York Cooking
- ❑ Ohio Cooking
- ❑ Pennsylvania Cooking
- ❑ Wisconsin Cooking
- ❑ Amish Mennonite Apple Cookbook
- ❑ Amish Mennonite Berry Cookbook
- ❑ Amish Mennonite Peach Cookbook
- ❑ Amish Mennonite Pumpkin Cookbook
- ❑ Amish & Mennonite Strawberry Cookbook
- ❑ Apples! Apples! Apples!
- ❑ Apples Galore
- ❑ Basil A-Z
- ❑ Berries! Berries! Berries!
- ❑ Berries Galore!
- ❑ Bountiful Blueberries

- ❑ Cherries! Cherries! Cherries!
- ❑ Cherries Galore
- ❑ Citrus! Citrus! Citrus!
- ❑ Cooking Beef, Pork & Lamb with Wine
- ❑ Cooking Seafood & Poultry with Wine
- ❑ Cooking with Asparagus
- ❑ Cooking with Cider
- ❑ Cooking with Fresh Basil
- ❑ Cooking with Fresh Herbs
- ❑ Cooking with Garlic
- ❑ Cooking with Spirits
- ❑ Cooking with Sweet Onions
- ❑ Cooking with Wine
- ❑ Cooking with Things Go Baa
- ❑ Cooking with Things Go Cluck
- ❑ Cooking with Things Go Moo
- ❑ Cooking with Things Go Oink
- ❑ Cooking with Things Go Splash
- ❑ Crazy for Basil
- ❑ Crockpot Cooking
- ❑ Good Cookin' From the Plain People
- ❑ How to Make Salsa
- ❑ Kid Cookin'
- ❑ Kid Fun
- ❑ Kid Money
- ❑ Kid Pumpkin Fun Book
- ❑ Midwest Small Town Cookin'
- ❑ Muffins Cookbook (Veggies, Fruit, Nut)

- ❑ Nuts! Nuts! Nuts!
- ❑ Off To College Cookbook
- ❑ Peaches! Peaches! Peaches!
- ❑ Pecans! Pecans! Pecans!
- ❑ Pumpkins! Pumpkins! Pumpkins!
- ❑ Recipes for Appetizers & Beverages Using Wine
- ❑ Recipes for Desserts Using Wine
- ❑ Some Like It Hot
- ❑ Soup's On!
- ❑ Southwest Cooking
- ❑ Squash Cookbook
- ❑ Super Simple Cookin'
- ❑ To Take the *Gamey* out of the Game Cookbook
- ❑ Working Girl Cookbook

Larger Mini Cookbooks
176 - 204 pages - $6.95

- ❑ Cooking with Mulling Spices
- ❑ Grass-Fed Beef Recipes
- ❑ Holiday & Get-Together Cookbook
- ❑ Veggie Talk Coloring & Story Book

In-Between Cookbooks
(5 1/2 x 8 1/2) - 150 pages - $9.95

- ❑ Adaptable Apple Cookbook
- ❑ Amish Ladies Cookbook - Old Husbands
- ❑ Amish Ladies Cookbook - Young Husbands
- ❑ Baseball Moms' Cookbook
- ❑ Basketball Moms' Cookbook
- ❑ Bird Up! Pheasant Recipes
- ❑ Buffalo Cookbook

- Camp Cookin'
- Catfish Cookin' Cookbook
- Civil War Cookin', Stories, 'n Such
- Cookin' Panfish Cookbook
- Cooking Ala Nude
- Cooking for a Crowd
- Cooking with Beer
- Country Cooking
  Recipes from my Amish Heritage
- Cow Puncher's Cookbook
- Das Hausbarn Cookbook
- Eating Ohio
- Farmers Market Cookbook
- Feast of Moons Indian Cookbook
- Fire Fighters Cookbook
- Football Mom's
- Funky Duck Cookbook
- Halloween Fun Book
- Herbal Cookery
- Hunting in the Nude Cookbook
- Ice Cream Cookbook
- Indian Cooking Cookbook
- Kids No Cook Cookbook

- Little 'Ol Blue-Haired Church-Lady
  Cookbook
- Mad About Garlic
- Make the Play All-Sport Cookbook
- Mountain Man Cookbook
- New Cooks' Cookbook
- No-Stove, No-Sharp Knife Kids' Cookbook
- Now, Whadda You Gonna Do With
  That Dead Deer Cookbook
- Outdoor Cooking for Outdoor Men
- Plantation Cookin' Cookbook
- Pumpkin Patch, Proverbs & Pies
- Shhh Cookbook
- Soccer Mom's Cookbook
- Southwest Ghost Town Cookbook
- Southwest Native American Cookbook
- Southwest Vegetarian Cookbook
- Trailer Trash Cookbook
- Turn of the Century Cooking
- Vegan Vegetarian Cookbook
- Venison Cookbook

Biggie Cookbooks
(5 1/2 x 8 1/2) - 200 plus pages - $11.95
- A Cookbook for them what Ain't Done
  a Whole lot of Cookin'
- Aphrodisiac Cooking
- Back to the Supper Table Cookbook
- Cooking for One (ok, Maybe two)
- Covered Bridges Cookbook
- Depression Times Cookbook
- Dial-a-Dream Cookbook
- Discover the Phillipines Cookbook
- Flat Out, Dirt Cheap Cookin'
- I-Got-Funner-Things-To Do Cookbook
- Hormone Helper Cookbook
- Mississippi River Cookbook
- Real Men Cook on Sunday Cookbook
- Southern Homemade Cooking
- Spice 'N Wine Cookbook
- Taste of Las Vegas Cookbook
- Vegetarian Wild Game Cookbook
- Victorian Sunday Dinners
- Wild Critter Cookbook

HEARTS 'N TUMMIES COOKBOOK CO.
3544 Blakslee St. • Wever, Iowa 52658
1-800-571-2665

Name _____

Address _____

_____ _____ Ph.# _____

*You Iowa folks gotta kick in another 6% for Sales Tax.